A true delight for readers young and old, *Piki Goes Flying* delivers a humorous retelling of Piki's first airplane flight. With a simple text structure and explanation of key vocabulary throughout, Joan M. Hellquist shares a valuable experience about inclusive travel, along with themes of safety and cooperation, while showcasing her bond with her very own Service Dog.

This book would serve as a wonderful instructional read aloud in any elementary school classroom.

**Rdepaola**
**LitPick**


Joan M. Hellquist creates a fine story filled with details about Piki's training and exposure to unfamiliar sights and sounds.

Libraries and adults looking for stories that educate all ages about Service Dog training, activities and methods of support will find *Piki Goes Flying* an attractive illustration of all these subjects.

**Diane Donovan**
**Midwest Book Review**


*Piki Goes Flying* serves dual purposes. It entertains and educates listeners. Joan includes up-to-date information about traveling on a plane with a Service Dog, including rules and regulations from the U.S. Department of Transportation and airlines.

**Kameron Brook**
**Reedsy Discovery**

# Piki Goes Flying

## Piki's Second Adventure

(Remember, Piki rhymes with sneaky!)

### Joan M. Hellquist

Author and Illustrator

# Piki Goes Flying

## Piki's Second Adventure

Copyright © 2022  Joan M. Hellquist
All rights reserved
ISBN 9798985761702
All Illustrations © Joan M. Hellquist

The Sunport name and logo is a registered trademark of the City of Albuquerque and is used with its permission.

Permission to use the Jetport name and logo was given by the Jetport Director

Any duplication or distribution of this work, in whole or in part without the express written permission of Joan M. Hellquist is prohibited.

**Other books by Joan M. Hellquist**

Hellquist, Joan M. *Beyond the Stars: The Other Side Through a Child's Eyes*. 2016.

Hellquist, Joan M. *Piki Goes to College*. 2021.

I knew something was up because Joan had her bags, that she calls suitcases, on the floor in her bedroom very close to my crate. She was putting clothes, shoes and other stuff into them. Joan had done this before and the day after she took the bags out of the house, she would disappear for days, sometime weeks but she always came back. I didn't understand why she didn't take me with her, so I felt left out. I kept a close eye on the bags to be sure she didn't leave me behind the next time she left.

This time, however, something else was happening. She put two rows of three chairs side by side out in the courtyard. The second row was very close to the first row and the third chair in each row was against the wall. This all seemed rather odd to me, but I figured Joan knew what she was doing.

A few days later, we went out to those chairs. Joan had me on a leash and she'd sidestep to the third chair of the second row. She urged me to come to her. There wasn't much space but being sort of long and lanky, I was able to get to her. Then Joan sat down in that chair and tried to get me to lie down in front of her with part of me under the chair in front of hers. Before I figured out what she wanted, I'd just lie down between the rows. Finally after a few days, I got the idea.

Once I knew what I was supposed to do, she'd let me go in first so I could curl up on the brick and then she would come sit down and put her feet on both sides of me. You would probably be surprised how little space I take up when I curl up on the floor. I was proud to have learned a new lesson, one I'd not been taught in college. But I had no idea when I would need to do this. It didn't make any sense to me.

Joan began taking me to the airport in Albuquerque. I'd never been there before. It is a very big place with a lot of parking lots on top of each other, like layers on a cake. Across the street there is a big building and beyond that was a wide open flat area that looks like a huge field of cement.

Every now and then, the things I'd seen flying over the house were coming out of the sky and sliding across the cement field. I had always thought they must be tiny birds when I'd see them over the house, but they didn't flap their wings. Joan explained to me that these things sliding on the cement field were airplanes, or planes. Although these airplanes sliding on the cement field were the same as the tiny ones in the sky, they looked a lot bigger here because they were much closer to us.

Joan and I went in the main door of the airport and then we took an elevator up to another floor. I'd been on an elevator before this. When we got out of the elevator, there were shops and restaurants all around us with lots of good smells coming from them. When Joan and I were in the middle of this very big room walking in a direction where there were no shops, something strange was happening and I couldn't take my eyes off of it.

There were people coming head first out of the floor! And a few feet beside them, people were disappearing into the floor feet first!

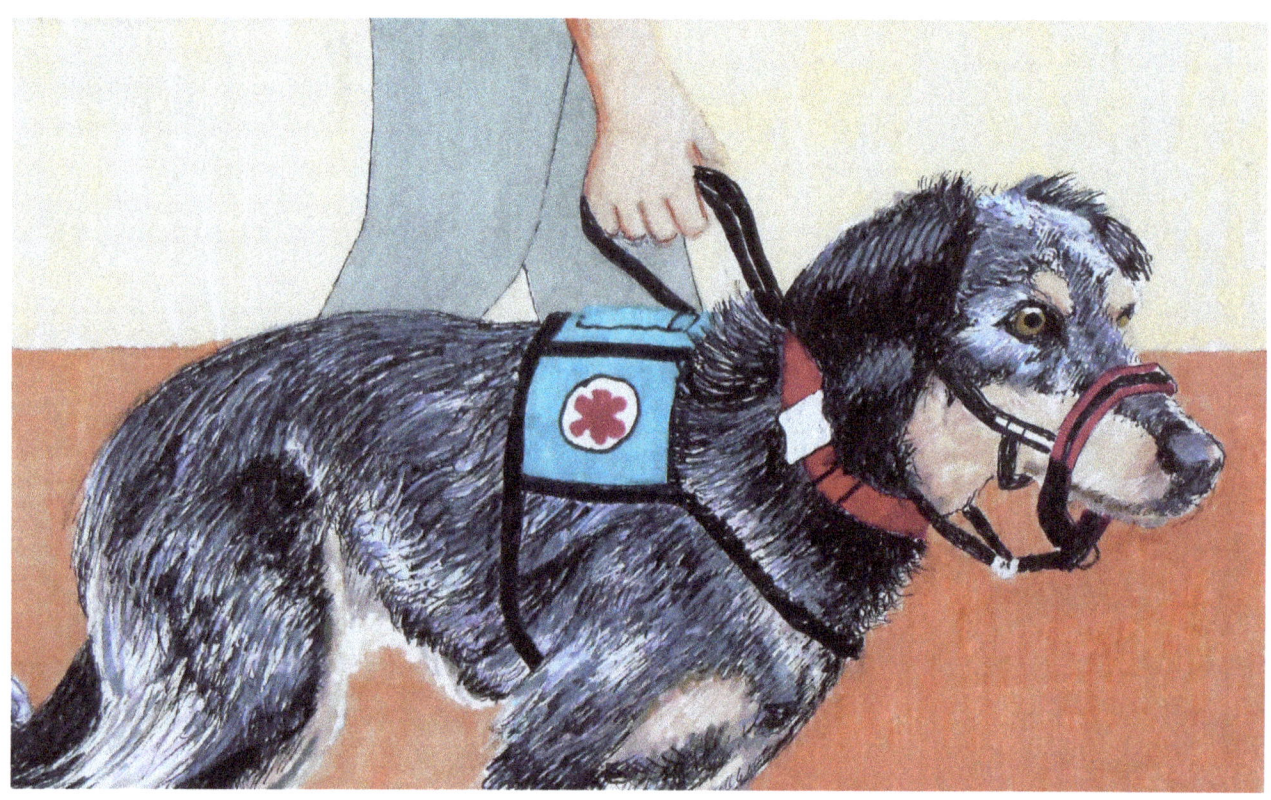

I thought it had to be magic, but Joan said it was the top of an escalator. We took the elevator back down one floor and I saw how it worked. It was moving stairs going up and beside them were moving stairs coming down.

Joan said that she would never take me on the escalator because my toenails could get caught in the metal grooves on the steps. It felt good to know that she was looking out for my safety.

There were lots of people on both floors of the airport. Many of them were standing in lines and they all had bags like Joan's bag that had little wheels on one end. The bags on wheels seemed to follow their person everywhere, just at their side. It looked like they had been trained to heel. I was very impressed and wondered how their person had trained a bag to heel. But it must be pretty easy to train them since it seemed like almost everyone had a heeling bag, even Joan.

Before we left the airport, Joan took me to a place that looked a lot like Joan's bathroom but was VERY BIG. There were many little rooms, like closets, along one side and many sinks across from the little rooms. We went into one of the little rooms and inside it looked like the corner of Joan's bathroom with that funny looking chair, like the one Joan has. It was pretty crowded in there but I could turn around so it wasn't a problem. What I really liked about the little room was that the walls and door didn't go down to the floor, so my tail could go underneath it. I also could look under the wall and see women's feet. There were feet in the little room right next to us and I guess my nose got under the wall. A lady said to me, "Hi Doggie." I thought that it was really nice of her to say hi to me.

Joan and I went back out into the layer cake parking lot, found Joan's car and went home. For a few weeks, Joan and I continued what I called "the lawn chair squeeze" and I got very good at it. But I still didn't know why we needed to do that.

We went back to the airport a few more times. Joan seemed to want to get me used to that place. I thought maybe the lawn chair squeeze had something to do with the airport, but we hadn't ever done it there. A couple of weeks later, Joan had finished packing her bags and put them in the trunk of her car. It was early the next morning that she put my gear on me. Oh, I was so excited! Joan drove us to Albuquerque very close to the airport and drove into a big parking lot. She was given a ticket by a person in a drive-by booth and then parked the car. As soon as Joan and I were out of the car, a small bright yellow bus drove up. The bus driver got the bags out of the trunk and put them in a closet at the back of the bus. Joan kept her backpack and we got on the bus with some other people.

When the bus stopped in front of the airport, the driver got everyone's bags out of the back of the little yellow bus. He got out one of Joan's bags and then the heeling one on wheels. But wait, he pushed a button on that bag and a long handle pulled out. Those bags that I thought were heeling on a leash were being pulled around by the people using that handle. I was glad to learn that bags aren't as smart and trainable as dogs!

We went inside, waited in a line and then went up to a counter where Joan showed a lady a little book and answered some questions about me. Then she put both of her bags on a flat surface next to the counter. The lady then gave Joan back her little book and some other papers.

After Joan gave the bags to the lady, we walked around the corner to that big room with the moving stairs at the end. We went to the elevator and up one floor. When we got out of the elevator, we were again in the room with the good smells. We passed a restaurant on the right and we went into another big room where Joan hadn't ever taken me. Again there were people in several different lines. Joan and I waited briefly in one line and when we were waved up to a small counter, a man in a uniform took the little book Joan had with a piece of paper in it. He looked at them, made a mark on one, handed them back to Joan and we got in a second line. This line was longer than the first one and we slowly made our way up to a long counter with gray plastic containers on it. People were putting all sorts of things like purses, phones, computers, jackets and even shoes into the plastic boxes. As we got up to that point, Joan used two of the gray plastic boxes to put her things into one and then took off my nose halter, vest and even my collar and put those in the other container! Why did Joan do that? I was now naked!

Joan slipped a braided plastic loop around my neck and we watched the two containers go on a moving counter into a machine that looked like an oven without a door. We moved over in front of a big doorway also without a door. The man on the other side of the doorway wanted me to go through the doorway to him, without Joan. I didn't know this man, why should I go to him? Joan seemed to want me to go through so she handed the end of the plastic loop to the man, who looked like he wasn't sure what to do. Then he stepped back and I went through the doorway with no door. Then Joan walked through and led me down to where the containers had come out of the oven thing. She put all my gear back on me and got her things. We walked out of that big room and I was glad. I didn't like that part of the airport at all!

Joan and I walked down a wide hallway to a sitting area with windows that looked out over the big cement field. This place was much nicer than the last place. I had all of my gear back on and I got a lot of attention from people sitting there. I could tell they liked me.

One of the airplane people opened a door in the outside wall and it looked like there was a tunnel on the other side of the door. We were allowed to walk down through the tunnel to get on the plane earlier than most of the people in the sitting area. I'm not sure why we got to get on the plane first with a few others, but I figured it was because we were special. As we got on the plane, two ladies in uniforms said hi to us. Wow, it was so exciting, I was going to go for a ride on a real airplane!

The inside of the plane had a long narrow path down the middle of it with three seats on both sides. Hmmm, three seats in a row with not much room between rows? Was this where I could show my lawn chair squeeze skills?

Because we got on the plane early, Joan could choose our seats. She and I stepped into the first row of three seats on the left. Joan sat down in the seat by the wall where there was a small window. Because it was the first row of seats on the plane, instead of seats in front of us, there was a wall with a carpet on it, called a bulkhead, and more room for me on the floor. Joan had to put her backpack into what they call "an overhead bin," above us. They seem to have special names for everything. We stayed there by the window as the rest of the people got on the plane. A nice lady got on and sat next to Joan. She seemed really friendly and happy to have me there. A few minutes later, a man sat down in the seat by the narrow path and the plane filled up.

One of the ladies who had met us at the door, stood in the long path next to the man two seats away. While another lady talked, I couldn't see where she was, the plane lady showed a wide leash kind of strap with a buckle, some cards, pointed at things including a drop-down plastic bag, draped a bright yellow plastic jacket around her neck, put a belt around her waist and blew into a little red tube. I had no idea why she did all of that. While she was doing that, the plane had backed up and started moving slowly down the edge of the big cement field.

Riding on the floor of the plane was sort of like riding on the floor of a car. But in the car I could see who was driving. I wanted to know who was driving this plane? And where was that person?

At the end of the cement field, the airplane turned around, the engines got really loud and the floor started to vibrate. Joan can tell you that I really don't like loud noises at all, so this made me very nervous. At first the plane went slowly but little by little, we went faster and faster as the engines got louder and louder and the vibrations worse. My ears felt clogged, and I wondered if I was going deaf.

All of a sudden the noise was much quieter, the vibrations stopped and it felt sort of like we were floating. We were floating. We were floating on air. We were flying!

The plane was up in the air flying for what seemed to be a long time. Joan talked with the lady beside her and I heard my name mentioned. I changed position a few times and curled up into a little ball. Joan always kept her feet beside me which helped to keep me calm and kept me out of the floorspace in front of the lady in the middle seat. Joan and I had practiced this at home and in restaurants.

The plane ladies and gentlemen came down the long path, the aisle, and gave drinks and tiny bags of treats to all of the people on the plane. They also told Joan how cute and well-behaved I was. I liked that, but they never offered me any treats! That didn't seem fair.

Every now and then I could hear a man talk, but I couldn't see him. I wondered if he was the driver. The third time he talked, something was different. The engines were making a slightly different sound and it seemed like maybe we weren't flying as high as we had been. I wanted to look out the window, but it was too high for me to see anything but sky.

The plane felt like we were slowing down. Then little by little my ears started feeling clogged again and I couldn't hear as well as usual. I hadn't gone deaf earlier, so I hoped I wouldn't this time either. Then all of a sudden I felt a big bump under the floor and I could tell we were now sliding on another big cement field. The plane's engines got really loud and the plane slowed down a lot.

Once we were almost stopped, the driver turned the plane around and we moved slowly back alongside the big cement field. The pressure in my ears got worse before we slid on the field, but now that we were no longer flying, I heard a crackling noise and I could hear again. Hooray! The driver turned the plane again, went forward a bit and then we stopped.

A few seconds later, I heard a little beep or bell sound and all of the passengers stood up and opened the little overhead closets, oh, sorry, overhead bins, and began to get their bags. The door that we had come through to get on the plane opened. Yippee, I thought, we're getting off the plane! I felt the people's excitement and my own too. When I ride with Joan in her car and we drive into a parking lot, I get really excited because I know we are going to get out. I've shown my excitement in the car and now on this airplane by whining. Joan calls my whining "squealing" and it is one of the things I do sometimes that Joan does not like, at all.

Joan gave me that look as if to say, "Why are you doing that? Please be quiet." Meanwhile the people around us said things like, "Oh, the poor dog," as if I was hurting or something. I got another look from Joan and although I continued to squeal, I tried to do it quietly.

Because we were in the front row, after the two people beside Joan left and one of the plane ladies gave Joan her backpack, we got out of our row. I quietly squealed all of the way out of the plane but quieted down as we walked through another long tunnel and came into a sitting area in a big building like the airport in Albuquerque.

I didn't know it, but we were going to get on a second plane in a couple of hours and Joan was concerned that I might need to pee. We were at a different airport and they had a dog relief area. To get to it we had to walk out of the airport, go down some stairs and ended up beside their layer cake parking lot to get to the relief area.

I can't say that this was a very welcoming place for a dog or a person. It was open air and overlooking the inside of one of the layers of the layer cake parking lot. It was made up of a fenced-in pen about sixteen feet square and the floor was covered with very green fake grass. It was nowhere near as inviting as real grass. It smelled like plastic and must be cleaned with some soap stuff. I couldn't tell if any other dog had used it recently. I guess that is good for the people that it is kept so clean, but not great for us dogs.

There was a little bench inside the fence at the edge of the fake grass, a poop scooper, poop bags, a covered container for the used poop bags and some spray stuff. I wondered if the spray was for cleaning the plastic grass. It was a strange place and I didn't do anything there. I'm sure that people would give it an "A" rating. But I'll give it an "N" rating, for NOT being anything like my backyard.

Joan and I went back into the airport to wait for our second airplane ride and, uh oh, there was another one of those places with the gray plastic boxes, moving counter, oven-like dark place and the doorway with no door. I had to get naked again, but I didn't have to walk through the doorway by myself. The TSA people, let Joan and I walk through together with me on the plastic loop leash. As we walked through the doorway, it made some sort of noise. We were then pulled aside where a lady had a metal stick that she moved around Joan's arms, legs, sides, front and back.

Then it was my turn to have the metal stick moved around me. Before the lady did that she asked Joan, "Will the dog bite me?" And Joan said that I wouldn't bite her and of course, I didn't. I stood still and let her move the metal stick around me. The metal stick, the lady called it a "wand," would beep if it found any metal on or in us. Joan had passed the wand test and it never beeped when the wand lady moved it around me either.

Joan's shoes had been looked at by someone else and he brought them back to her. The wand lady thought that the doorway without a door had beeped possibly because of something on Joan's shoes, like a cleaning product. Ah, ha, I thought that relief area smelled funny. Joan thought it might have beeped because she has an artificial hip.

Joan put my gear back on and we walked around the airport which had stores, restaurants, smells and lots of people, just like the airport in Albuquerque, only bigger. We sat down for a while and then went to a sitting area by the tunnel that led out to our plane. Now that I had done this once, I figured that I could handle it and hoped that there would be no surprises.

We got on that plane early and sat in exactly the same seats as we had sat on the first plane. Everyone else got on the plane but for some reason we couldn't leave right away. One of the plane ladies said we were delayed, but it wouldn't be for long, so everyone was to please stay seated. Shortly after that a man wearing a uniform and uniform hat came out of the room at the very front of the plane. His uniform was really fancy looking with shiny metal buttons, lots of gold stripes on his shoulders and a pair of wings on the left side of the front of his jacket. The plane ladies called him "Captain" and he came over to our row. He saw me and asked Joan if this was the first time I'd ever flown. Joan said, "Yes." He then asked my name and Joan told him, Piki, and spelled it for him. The man smiled, welcomed us and walked out through the tunnel.

The man in the uniform, the Captain, came back onto the plane about ten minutes later and gave Joan a paper with something attached to it. He smiled at me again and said, "Piki, this is for you." Joan thanked him and he went back into the little room in the front of the plane. Joan showed me the paper. It was a welcome to my first flight on an airplane, which had my name on it and was signed by him, the plane gentlemen and the plane ladies, otherwise known as the crew. And best of all, attached at the top were wings like the Captain had on his uniform jacket! I didn't receive a tiny bag of treats like the other passengers, but I was the only one to receive wings from the Captain!

Joan explained that the man, the Captain, is the pilot. That's airplane talk for driver. Wow, and he gave me my very own wings! Oh, and the little room in the front is called the cockpit and the plane ladies and men are called flight attendants. I learned a lot of new words that day. A few minutes later, my friend, the Captain, started the plane, backed out, slowly drove down along the big cement field, turned around and then went very fast until we went up into the air.

Here are some more vocabulary words that you might already know. The pilot has a helper in the cockpit who also wears wings and is called the co-pilot. Now that I had my own wings, I wondered if I could be a co-pilot. Well, probably not since I knew nothing about flying a plane. I'm sure the co-pilot, like the pilot, had lots of training.

To drive the plane slowly on the ground is to taxi. The big cement field from which the plane goes up into the air is called the runway. To go up into the air is taking off. To come back down on the runway is landing and to go from one airport to another on a plane is called a flight.

This flight was very much like the first one. My ears felt clogged going up, the flight attendants served drinks and little bags of treats to everyone but me, my ears crackled and cleared as we got closer to the new airport. We landed and my friend the Captain taxied the plane to the gate, another new word.

The plane stopped, people got up and were excited like they were when we landed the first time. And what did I do, well, I squealed, not very loudly, but continuously. These passengers were concerned about me too and Joan was staring at me again. She look embarrassed. I know, as a Service Dog, there are a lot of things I am not supposed to do on an airplane, but I just got excited and made my high-pitched squealing noise. During both flights I was totally quiet, so except for the people in our row and the crew, no one else realized there was a dog on the plane until after we landed.

While getting off the plane, deplaning, and after I stopped the quiet squeal, I asked Joan about the place called security, where I have to go through naked. The people there have the initials TSA on their uniforms. I asked what those initials stand for and she told me they stand for Transportation Security Administration.

After Joan and I got off the plane, through the tunnel and into the airport, we then went to a place called Baggage Claim. Baggage Claim was a long rubber mat that moved around and everyone's bags appeared one by one through a hole in the wall and onto the moving mat. Joan grabbed her bags and we went to another count-er called Car Rental. She did some paperwork again and then we went out to their layer cake parking lot called a parking garage. We got into the car that Joan just rented, she attached a short leash to my collar and then clicked it into where the seatbelt attaches to the seat.

I was used to riding in a car so this part of the trip was easy for me. Joan will tell you that I wasn't always well behaved in a car. When we would go to Rick and Heather's for training, I would lunge forward between the two front seats repeatedly and squealed, but this squealing was A LOT louder than my airplane squealing. At that time, screaming was the term that Joan used for it. But I'm over that now and I ride very nicely in the car. Yes, I still do some of the airplane squeal when Joan drives into parking lots that I recognize. It is difficult to behave perfectly.

One of the flight attendants had told us when we were landing that we were landing in Portland, Maine. The only thing I knew about it was that I had never been there before. I don't know if you know this, but every airport is given a three letter code name. I saw on Joan's bags that they had a tag on them with the letters PWM. That is the three letter name identifying the Portland, Maine airport. I can see the P is for Portland and the M is for Maine, but what does the W stand for?

As we drove away from the PWM airport, Joan made a comment about how this place is called a Jetport rather than an airport. It was the Portland International Jetport. I guess that means only jets can fly in and out of there. There are other kinds of planes, Joan told me. I wonder what the Jetport has against those other planes?

And then I remembered Joan telling me that the airport in Albuquerque, (ABQ, now that makes sense,) is called a Sunport. What does that mean? Isn't there only one sun and we do get a lot of sunny days there, but the sun doesn't land there. So I guess Jetport isn't too odd.

Our drive from the airport to where we were going, our destination, was really pretty and nice. We saw lots of tall trees, fields filled with big gray rocks and pitched roofed houses, some actually attached to barns. We crossed both fast moving rivers and slow rivers that were shallow and clear so that you could see the sandy bottoms. There were also lots of well-kept gardens with brightly colored flowers. The air was much cooler than in New Mexico where we live, and you couldn't see very far because of all of the trees. It was sort of like the exact opposite of New Mexico, but I really liked it in this new place too.

One thing about this place that was strange to me was that there were LOTS of places along the road that had big signs out front advertising either ICE CREAM or DONUTS. We have ice cream and donuts in New Mexico, but nowhere near as many places that sell them. People who live here must really love ice cream and donuts.

I didn't know where we were, other than some place near Portland, Maine. Nor did I know where we were going. I'm not going to tell you where we ended up since that is where my next adventure takes place and that is the subject of my next book. So I'm sorry, but you'll just have to wait for Piki's Third Adventure.

It has been fun visiting with you again. I hope you have learned some things about flying with a Service Dog and thanks for listening.

Bye for now,

Piki, SD

Service Dog

# P. S. from Piki

### Why did I have to learn the "Lawn Chair Squeeze?"

Do you remember me telling you at the beginning of this adventure before we went on this trip, that Joan had me crowding in between rows of chairs and even partially under the chairs, doing the lawn chair squeeze? Because we sat in bulkhead seats on both of these first two flights, I didn't have to do that. But since that trip, I've had to use what she taught me so that I could fit at her feet when she's sitting in a regular seat, which is much more crowded than a bulkhead seat. I'm so glad she thought to get me trained ahead of time. If we hadn't practiced at home, I would probably have been very frightened to first get into that small space on a plane.

### Why are the code letters for the Portland International Jetport PWM? What does the W represent? And why is it called a Jetport?

I asked Joan about this after our trip and she looked it up for me. The code letters, PWM, come from the time when pilots followed lights from airport to airport. The last light before Portland was in the town of Westport, ME so the Jetport back then was called Portland-Westport-Municipal. The W stands for Westport and the M for Municipal., not Maine. That is why the Portland International Jetport is PWM.

In the late 1960s the runways were lengthened so that jets could land there. In June 1968, a headline in a local opinion column read, "Maine Joins The Jet Age," and the airport became the Jetport.

## Why is the Airport in Albuquerque called a Sunport?

Joan wasn't able to get much information by looking on the internet to explain why the Albuquerque airport is called the Albuquerque International Sunport. While getting permission to use the logo of the Sunport in this book, she corresponded with two men who work there. She asked them my question and this is the answer she received.

As the story goes, in 1963 there was a naming contest for the airport. A man named Harley Townsend, who was a pilot, won the contest with his entry of "Sunport." Joan was told he thought that Sunport was a good name because Albuquerque gets an average of 280 days of sun a year and he liked the sound of Sunport over his airplane radio. So in 1963, the official name was the Albuquerque Sunport.

In 1971 when the Sunport gained international status, the name was changed to the Albuquerque International Airport. And finally in 1994, it became the Albuquerque International Sunport!

**Joan, Teddy and Piki**

Joan M. Hellquist and her friends and family Teddy and Piki are happy to present this third of Joan's children's books and Piki's second book.

Joan lives in Placitas, New Mexico and spends some time in New Hampshire during the summer months. She is a retired Physician Assistant and is presently writing, drawing illustrations and painting a portrait of her five year old grandniece, Anna. Joan also works with 8-10 year olds as a volunteer bereavement facilitator at The Grief Center in Albuquerque. She has had a lifelong love for children, animals, art, traditional music, the wilderness and travel.

To contact Joan, please go to her website
**www.joanmhellquistAE.com**

In Loving Memory
of
**Teddy**

20?? - November 25, 2022

# Let Me Introduce to You, my Doggie Cousins

**Boomer
aka "Boomie"**

Australian Cattle Dog

Member of the
C. Eric Hellquist Family

**Ender**
Standard Poodle

Member of the
Paul T. Hellquist Family
and a
Service Dog

(like me, Piki)

# Mom, Dad, Teachers, Librarians and Other Adults

Although this is a children's book, as I did with Piki's first book, *Piki Goes to College,* I'm including information for adults since I want this to be an educational book for adults as well as a fun book for children.

There has been so much in the media about people trying to pass their pet off as a service or emotional support animal on an airline flight. Because of people abusing this right by trying to pass their pet peacock or pig off as a trained service animal, the U.S. Department of Transportation got together with others who deal with service animals flying on airlines. They changed some of the rules and came up with a Final Rule on Traveling by Air with Service Animals in December 2020. The next four pages are directly from the U.S. DOT website and include the new rules and the Final Rule. There are also additional rules from airlines and my personal recommendations.

For more information on traveling by air with a service animal, please go to **www.transportation.gov**. Search for "service animals" and you will see several articles available. The site has so much in it that it can be a bit confusing, but all of the information is there and can be downloaded, including the two forms that are mentioned on the next page.

# Final Rule on Traveling by Air with Service Animals
Announced by U.S. DOT, December 2, 2020

Defines a service animal as a dog that is individually trained to do work or perform tasks for the benefit of a person with a disability (Under the Air Carrier Access Act, a service animal means a dog only)

No longer considers an emotional support animal to be a service animal

Requires airlines to treat psychiatric service animals the same as other service animals

Allows airlines to require forms developed by the DOT attesting to a service animal's health, behavior and training and if taking a long flight attesting that the service animal can either not relieve itself, or can relieve itself in a sanitary manner during the flight (The Service Animal Health, Behavior, Training Form and The Service Animal Relief Attestation Form)

Allows airlines to require individuals traveling with a service animal to provide the DOT service animal form(s) up to 48 hours in advance of the date of travel if the passenger's reservation was made prior to that time

Prohibits airlines from requiring passengers with a disability who are traveling with a service animal to physically check-in at the airport instead of using the online check-in process

Allows airlines to require a person with a disability seeking to travel with a service animal to provide the DOT service animal form(s) at the passenger's departure gate on the date of travel.

Allows airlines to limit the number of service animals traveling with a single passenger with a disability to two service animals

Allows airlines to require a service animal to fit within its handler's foot space on the aircraft

## Other Information on Service Animals from U. S. DOT

**Airlines are permitted to deny transport to a service dog if it:**

Violates safety requirements e.g., too large or heavy to be accommodated in the cabin

Poses a direct threat to the health or safety of others

Causes a significant disruption in the cabin or at airport gate areas

Violates health requirements e.g., prohibited from entering a U.S. territory or foreign country

Airlines may also deny transport to a service dog if the airline requires completed DOT service animal forms and the service animal user does not provide the airline these forms

# Some additional individual airline rules for traveling with a service dog

Service animal must be clean and well-behaved

The service animal must be able to sit at your feet, under the seat in front of you, or if the service animal is smaller than a two year old child, the dog may sit in your lap.

**Service animals may not:**

Be seated in an exit row

Protrude into or block aisles

Occupy a seat

Block any passenger from getting out of the row, in other words the handler must sit in a window seat.

Eat from a tray table

**If your service is too large or heavy to be accommodated in the cabin, you may need to:**

Rebook on a flight with more open seats

Buy a ticket for the animal

Transport the animal as a checked pet

## Airlines can determine whether an animal is a service animal or pet by:

Asking an individual if they have a disability, if the animal is required to accompany the passenger because of the disability and what work or task the animal has been trained to perform

Looking for physical indicators such as the presence of a harness or vest

Looking to see if the animal is leashed or otherwise tethered

Observing the behavior of the animal (and the handler)

## Joan's best recommendations for airline travel with a Service Dog are very simple

Be sure as you head to the airport that you have all of your Service Dog's gear, equipment, food, water, food and/or water dish, poop bags, ALL of the things that you could possibly need. (Airports are full of shops with things you might need for yourself, but not things you might need for your Service Dog.)

Get to the airport EARLY, at least an hour earlier than you get there when traveling alone.

Be sure to check with the airline you are flying on, prior to the day of your flight, to see if they have any of their own special rules.

www.ingramcontent.com/pod-product-compliance
Lightning Source LLC
LaVergne TN
LVHW070529070526
838199LV00073B/6733